KU-555-766

Cork City Library

WITHDRAWN
FROM STOCK

JADEN SMITH

Clare Hibbert

LONDON·SYDNEY

First published in 2012 by
Franklin Watts
338 Euston Road
London NW1 3BH

Franklin Watts Australia
Level 17/207 Kent Street
Sydney NSW 2000

Copyright © Franklin Watts 2012

All rights reserved.

Series editor: Adrian Cole
Art direction: Peter Scoulding
Design: Simon Borrough
Picture research: Diana Morris

Acknowledgements:
Action Press/Rex Features: 29. Agencia EFE/Rex Features: 26.
BDG/Rex Features: 22. © Buy Life: 28. Brian Cahn/Zuma Press/Corbis: 25.
Gilbert Carrasquillo/Getty Images: 27.
Michael Caulfield/WireImages/Getty Images: 24.
Columbia Pictures/Everett/Rex Features: 12, 23.
D Free/Shutterstock: 4. Jacob de Golish/Getty Images: 15b.
Steve Granitz/Wirephoto/Getty Images: front cover.
It's A Laugh Productions/Walt Disney TV/Kobal Collection: 18.
Chris Jackson/Getty Images: 21. KPA/Zuma/Rex Features: 5.
Dave Lewis/Rex Features: 7. Kevin Mazur/WireImages/Getty Images: 11.
Most Wanted/Rex Features: 8, 15t. Overbrook Entertainment/Warner Brothers: 10.
Rex Features: 20. Startracks Photo/Rex Features: 6.
20th Century Fox/Everett/Rex Features: 16, 17.

Every attempt has been made to clear copyright. Should there be any inadvertent
omission please apply to the publisher for rectification.

A CIP catalogue record for this book
is available from the British Library.

Dewey Classification: 791.4'3'028'092

ISBN: 978 1 4451 0660 1

Printed in China

Franklin Watts is a division of Hachette
Children's Books, an Hachette UK company.
www.hachette.co.uk

Contents

Words highlighted in the text can be found in the glossary.

Cool customer

Jaden Smith is one of Hollywood's hottest young talents. He made his name as a child actor in *The Pursuit of Happyness* and *The Karate Kid*. He's a cool rapper and dancer, too. It's helped having mega-star parents, of course – Jaden's dad is Will Smith and his mum is Jada Pinkett Smith.

"I'd say my dad is the best actor in the family because he has been doing it the longest and he's had more work."

Jaden Smith (on left) with his sister, dad and mum in 2009.

Jaden has inherited his acting and musical skills from his parents – and also owes his amazing good looks to them. Will Smith is African-American, while Jada's background includes African-Caribbean, **Creole** and Portuguese-Jewish **ancestry**.

Jaden had a great start to life being born into such a supportive family. Here he is in 2008.

He may be "Dad" to Jaden, but to the general public Will Smith is a top actor who's been nominated for two Oscars and won multiple Grammy Awards. His films include *I, Robot* and *Men in Black*.

Family ties

Jaden's parents first met in 1990 when Jada auditioned to play Will's girlfriend in his hit TV show, *The Fresh Prince of Bel-Air*. She didn't land the role, but she did win her prince in the end. Will and Jada were married on New Year's Eve 1997.

Jaden, aged 4, with his mum and dad.

Jaden Christopher Syre Smith was born on 8 July 1998 in Malibu, California. His mum took on fewer acting roles so she could spend time with her son, saying: "I'd rather not star in anything right now because I need to be flexible for my family."

Jaden's little sister Willow arrived on 31 October 2000. Jaden and Willow have an older half-brother, Trey, who is Will's son from his first marriage.

Will and Jada with their baby daughter Willow.

❝Both my dad and mom give me advice about acting, [like], 'You have to stay in the scene. No matter what happens, you got to stay in the scene.'❞

Homes, sweet
homes

Home for Jaden is a nine-bedroom adobe mansion in Malibu. Jaden's mum told *Architectural Digest* how she "wanted to create a family retreat, something made by hand and as natural as possible".

Swimming pool

Volleyball court

Main house

Tennis court

Basketball court

Not many young teens are lucky enough to have 40 hectares to run around in! Jaden's Malibu "garden" includes tennis, basketball and sand volleyball courts, a pool, and batting cages where he can practise his baseball skills.

"I'm going to buy my parents' house ... I'm going to give them a little apartment."

The Malibu mansion is just one of the homes owned by the Smith family. Others include a waterfront mansion in Miami Beach.

Jaden's Malibu home from the air. The complex is thought to be worth around £12.5 million.

Jaden's parents both came from hard-working backgrounds and encourage their kids not to take their millionaire lifestyle for granted. Will has passed on to Jaden his great-grandmother's favourite saying: "Don't let failure go to your heart and don't let success go to your head."

Life on TV

It was only a matter of time before Jaden would follow his parents into acting. He first appeared on television when he was just five years old.

The show was the US sitcom *All of Us*, whose creators were Will and Jada. Giving him a small part allowed Jaden's parents to spend time with their boy when they were on set as **writer-producers**.

Jaden starred as Reggie in the US TV series *All of Us*.

Will and Jada co-created *All of Us* with Betsy Borns. Betsy made her name producing such **blockbusting** TV series as *Roseanne* and *Friends*.

Jaden and his dad at the Kids' Choice Awards in 2003.

All of Us was about a separated couple and their young son, Bobby Jr, played by Khamani Griffin. Jaden appeared in six episodes as one of Bobby Jr's friends and rivals, Reggie. In one classic episode, "Boxing", Jaden and Khamani try to rap. When Jaden has trouble finding a rhyme for "Reggie", Khamani helpfully suggests "wedgie"!

First film

Jaden's first movie was *The Pursuit of Happyness*, released in December 2006. He played Christopher Jr, the son of a salesman who loses everything.

The movie was based on the true story of Chris Gardner, who ended up in a homeless shelter with his son while learning to be a stockbroker as an unpaid **intern**.

A scene from *The Pursuit of Happyness,* in which Jaden and Will were cast as son and father.

Will Smith played Gardner. Being father and son in real life made the on-screen **chemistry** easy. One critic praised Jaden as "a chip off the old block, uncommonly at ease before the cameras."

"You know what wasn't fun? That he [Will] was always in character. We'd be in the trailer and I'd be like, 'Dad, can I have an orange juice?' and he'd be like 'Sorry Christopher, we can't afford an orange juice!'"

Jaden won an MTV Movie Award for "Best Newcomer" for his role in *The Pursuit of Happyness*. Will received Oscar and Golden Globe nominations for his role.

School days

Jaden's career as a child actor hasn't stopped him keeping up with his studies. At first he was taught by his mum and a home tutor, so he could have his lessons on set.

In 2008, Will and Jada opened the New Village Leadership Academy in Calabasas, California. As well as offering traditional subjects, such as numeracy and literacy, there were classes in karate, yoga and etiquette (manners). Both Jaden and his sister Willow went there.

Jaden inherited his maths skills from his dad. Will did a course in engineering at the Massachusetts Institute of Technology before becoming a hip-hop MC.

The New Village
Leadership Academy
in Calabasas, California.

Jaden's half-brother
Trey graduated from
Oaks Christian School
in Westlake Village in
June 2011. Trey (right)
had been on the school
football team, and
Jaden and his dad
often supported Trey
at inter-school matches.
On one occasion, Jaden
took his celeb friends
Justin Bieber and Selena
Gomez to a game!

Blockbuster!

Jennifer Connelly, Jaden Smith and Keanu Reeves in a scene from *The Day the Earth Stood Still*.

In 2008, director **Scott Derrickson** remade the classic 1950s sci-fi film, *The Day the Earth Stood Still*. **Top billing went to Keanu Reeves, playing a humanoid alien called Klaatu, and Jennifer Connelly, as scientist Helen Benson.**

Jaden took the part of Helen's son, Jacob. Jaden's character has to trust his mum's judgement that Klaatu is out to help, not to threaten. Keanu was impressed by how Jaden handled the role: "He was very professional. It was his second movie. He takes his work very seriously."

16

> **"One of the things I'm gonna remember most about working on *The Day the Earth Stood Still* is the smell of the fog. I mean you had like this kinda like gassy thing in the fog ... it was really weird."**

Characters Helen and Jacob are caught up in events after the arrival of aliens on Earth.

Keanu Reeves first met Jaden years earlier, on the set of the *Matrix* movies. Jaden's mum Jada starred as Captain Niobe in the **trilogy**, while Keanu was Neo.

Life is "suite"

All young stars know they've made it when they're asked to appear on the Disney Channel's *The Suite Life of Zack & Cody*. Jaden's invite came in 2008 and he made the most of it, showing genuine wit and humour. As his dad once admitted: "This kid is funnier than I was at his age. But then, he did have me as a father."

In the episode, Jaden plays a boy called Travis who helps the twins to impress their girlfriends. He teaches Cody how to do karate and Zack how to cook a gourmet meal. In spite of all Travis does for them, Zack and Cody choose not to take him bowling on his last night in town – but they get their comeuppance. Their girlfriends stand *them* up and go out with Jaden's cute character instead!

Jaden's character, Travis, is measured up in *The Suite Life of Zack & Cody*.

"Lesson Number One: expect the unexpected."

Jaden as Travis in The Suite Life of Zack & Cody

Jaden appeared in *Zack & Cody* season 3, episode 18 – called "Romancing the Phone". Zack and Cody are played by real-life twins, Dylan and Cole Sprouse.

19

Friends in high places

By the end of 2009, Jaden was mixing in even more impressive company. President Barack Obama had been awarded the Nobel Peace Prize, and Jaden's parents were asked to host the Peace Prize Concert in Oslo, Norway.

Jaden visited Barack Obama's official residence, the White House, in April 2011 (below). His sister Willow was singing there as part of the annual Easter Egg Roll festivities.

The whole Smith family performed at the concert. It was a massive event, with megastars such as Donna Summer, Wyclef Jean and Westlife all taking part. Jaden sang and danced brilliantly. Fans were as impressed by Jaden's looks as his performance. They gave a thumbs-up for his "big hair" – a departure from his usual braids.

Jaden and Willow sing alongside their mum and dad at the Peace Prize Concert in 2009.

Karate Kid

Jaden's karate kicks on *Zack & Cody* had been a taste of things to come. In 2010 he took top billing in a re-make of the 1984 hit, *The Karate Kid*. Excitingly, his co-star was the legendary Jackie Chan. "He was, like, the most amazing person ever!" said Jaden.

Jaden with martial arts star Jackie Chan at the 2010 MTV Movie Awards.

During filming, Jaden spent at least an hour and a half training every day. Learning to do the splits was one of the hardest moves!

"I knew all of Jackie's stuff. He and my dad are my two biggest influences. Jackie is really cool. Every time that he would come on set, he would say good morning in a different language. He was always teaching me new things."

This scene from takes place on the Great Wall of China.

Jaden played Dre Parker, who moves to China and is bullied at his new school. He learns self-defence from a kung fu master, Mr Han (Jackie Chan). Most filming was done on location in China – in the capital, Beijing, and in the beautiful Huangshan Mountains. Jaden enjoyed visiting China, but wasn't so keen on the local food. Mostly, he stuck to hamburgers!

Sweet charity

Jaden has it all – looks, fame and wealth – but he still finds time to give something back. As his mum once pointed out, "My kids are very willing to give things away because they understand that they have such abundance."

$10 BUYS THE ESSENTIAL HIV/AIDS CARE NECESSARY TO KEEP A CHILD OR ADULT WITH HIV/AIDS ALIVE FOR ONE WEEK.

WHEN YOU BUY LIFE, YOU GIVE LIFE. DOWNLOAD THE FREE APP AND SCAN THIS AD OR TEXT 'BUYLIFE' TO 90999 TO GIVE $10 AND BUY LIFE FOR THE MILLIONS AFFECTED BY HIV/AIDS IN AFRICA AND INDIA.

$10 will be added to your mobile phone bill, deducted from your prepaid account. Msg & data rates may apply. Reply STOP to 90999 to stop. Full terms: mGive.org/T. Keep a Child Alive is a registered 501c3 charity. Photograph of Jaden and Willow Smith by Markus Klinko & Indrani, styling by GK Reid. Suggested app: Wimo at getwimo.com.

keep a child alive

In October 2010 Jaden lent his support to Alicia Keys' Keep a Child Alive campaign. He wore one of its "Buy Life" T-shirts – a built-in barcode can be scanned with a smartphone to donate money to people with HIV/AIDS in Africa and India (see http://buylife.org/). Jaden is also a **youth ambassador** for Project Zambi, which raises awareness of poverty in Africa.

Will is proud of his son's charity work: "We call him an empath. He has the power to **empathise** with situations he has no knowledge of beforehand."

Jaden and Willow autographed model elephants (below) to help raise money for Project Zambi. Find out more about the partnership at www.projectzambi.org

Making

music

The theme tune to *The Karate Kid* movie was "Never Say Never", performed by Canadian heart throb Justin Bieber. Justin released the song as a single, and the accompanying video had footage of Justin and Jaden messing around in the studio.

> **"The tour is going to be swag."**

Jaden and Justin strike a pose during Justin's world tour in 2011.

26

In 2011, Jaden and Willow were each nominated for the BET Young Star Award. Thankfully, any brother-sister rivalry was avoided – it was awarded to them jointly!

Jaden's **collaboration** with Justin established his credentials as a super-cool musical artist. Jaden joined Justin's 2011 world tour and some of their dance-offs were breathtaking. Jaden appeared in Justin's 3-D film about the last leg of his Never Say Never tour along with the R&B "king", Usher, *Hannah Montana* star Miley Cyrus and hip-hop legend Snoop Dogg.

Willow and Jaden at the BET Awards, 2011.

Future films

With such talent, dedication and family support, it's not surprising that Jaden is facing a bright future. Top men's style magazine featured Jaden in a photoshoot in 2011. At 12 years old, he was the youngest star to have appeared in the magazine.

"I don't like movies that make you cry. But if girls like dramas, then I'll do it!"

Jaden signs his autograph for waiting fans.

Jaden certainly likes to keep it in the family. He's also in a movie called *Amulet*, based on a graphic novel by Kazu Kibuishi, which co-stars his sister.

Jaden is a great rapper, dancer and actor. In spring 2012 he was working on *After Earth*, a movie directed by M. Night Shymalan.

In the future, Jaden plans to keep working with his dad's production company, Overbrook. He's still got a lot of growing up to do, but he's perfectly placed to make the most of his acting and musical talent.

Jaden had his long hair cut in January 2012.

Fan guide

Full Name: Jaden Christopher Syre Smith
Date of birth: 8 July 1998
Height: 1.56 metres
Hometown: Malibu, California, USA
Star sign: Cancer
Colour of eyes: Brown
Hobbies: Wushu (martial art), basketball,
   eating pizza with friends

There are many sites about Jaden, and often they let you contribute to discussions about him. Remember, though, that it's OK to make comments, but it's not fair to be unkind. He cannot answer your comments himself!

http://www.jadensmith.com/

https://www.facebook.com/officialjaden

http://www.whosay.com/jadensmith

http://jaden-smith.net/

http://will-smith.net/category/jaden-smith/

http://www.youtube.com/officialjaden

http://www.imdb.com/name/nm1535523/

Please note: every effort has been made by the Publishers to ensure that these websites contain no inappropriate or offensive material. However, because of the nature of the Internet, it is impossible to guarantee that the contents of these sites will not be altered. We strongly advise that Internet access is supervised by a responsible adult.

8 July 1998	Jaden Christopher Syre Smith is born
2003–2004	Appears as Reggie in six episodes of *All of Us*
2006	Plays Christopher Jr in *The Pursuit of Happyness*
	Wins a Phoenix Film Critics Society Award for his performance as Christopher Jr
2007	Wins an MTV Movie Award and Teen Choice Award for *The Pursuit of Happyness*
	Co-presents two awards at the Oscars, along with actor Abigail Breslin
2008	Appears in *The Day the Earth Stood Still*
	Guest-stars on *The Suite Life of Zack & Cody*
	Appears in Alicia Keys' "Superwoman" video
2009	Becomes a youth ambassador for Project Zambi
	Sings at the Nobel Peace Prize Concert
2010	Stars in *The Karate Kid* with Jackie Chan
	Raps on Justin Bieber's single, "Never Say Never"
	Dances on the video for Willow's "Whip My Hair"
	Supports the "Keep a Child Alive" campaign
2011	Wins a Young Artist Award for his lead in *The Karate Kid*
	Nominated for two Black Reel Awards, an Empire Award and an MTV Movie Award
	Tours with Justin Bieber
	Becomes the youngest star featured in *GQ*
	Shares a BET Young Star Award with Willow
	Announces that he'll star in *Amulet*
	Records a cover of Frank Ocean's "Thinking of You" with Justin Bieber
2012	Agrees to star in *Karate Kid 2*
	Begins filming *After Earth*

CORK CITY LIBRARY

31

Glossary

Ancestry Family history.

Blockbusting Commercially successful.

Chemistry In this use of the word, when two people have a lot in common with each other.

Collaboration Work with someone.

Creole A descendant of a European or African person who settled in the West Indies.

Director The person in charge of making a film or TV show.

Empathise Be understanding of another's situation.

Intern On-the-job training.

Nominated Put forward for an award or position.

Trilogy Any group of three related books or films.

Writer-producer Someone who works on the script of a TV show or film, and who also works with the director to make it happen.

Youth ambassador A young person who represents a particular charity.

Index